ASTROLOGY

CAPRICORN

BY ABBY DOTY

Apex is distributed by North Star Editions:
sales@northstareditions.com | 888-417-0195

Produced for Apex by Red Line Editorial.

Photographs ©: Shutterstock Images, cover (illustration, constellation), cover (background), 1, 4–5, 6, 8, 9, 10–11, 12–13, 15, 19, 20, 21, 22–23, 26, 27; Eva Hambach/AFP/Getty Images, 14; iStockphoto, 16–17, 29; Tim Clayton/Corbis Sport/Getty Images, 24–25

Library of Congress Control Number: 2025939150

ISBN
979-8-89250-783-7 (hardcover)
979-8-89250-812-4 (paperback)
979-8-89250-869-8 (ebook pdf)
979-8-89250-841-4 (hosted ebook)

Printed in the United States of America
Mankato, MN
012026

NOTE TO PARENTS AND EDUCATORS

Apex books are designed to build literacy skills in striving readers. Exciting, high-interest content attracts and holds readers' attention. The text is carefully leveled to allow students to achieve success quickly. Additional features, such as bolded glossary words for difficult terms, help build comprehension.

TABLE OF CONTENTS

CHAPTER 1

THE SEA GOAT

Several dim stars form an arrowhead shape. It's the Capricornus **constellation**. The front part looks like a goat. But it has the tail of a fish.

CAPRICORNUS

Capricornus's brightest star, Deneb Algedi, is at one end of the arrowhead shape. It helps form the fish tail.

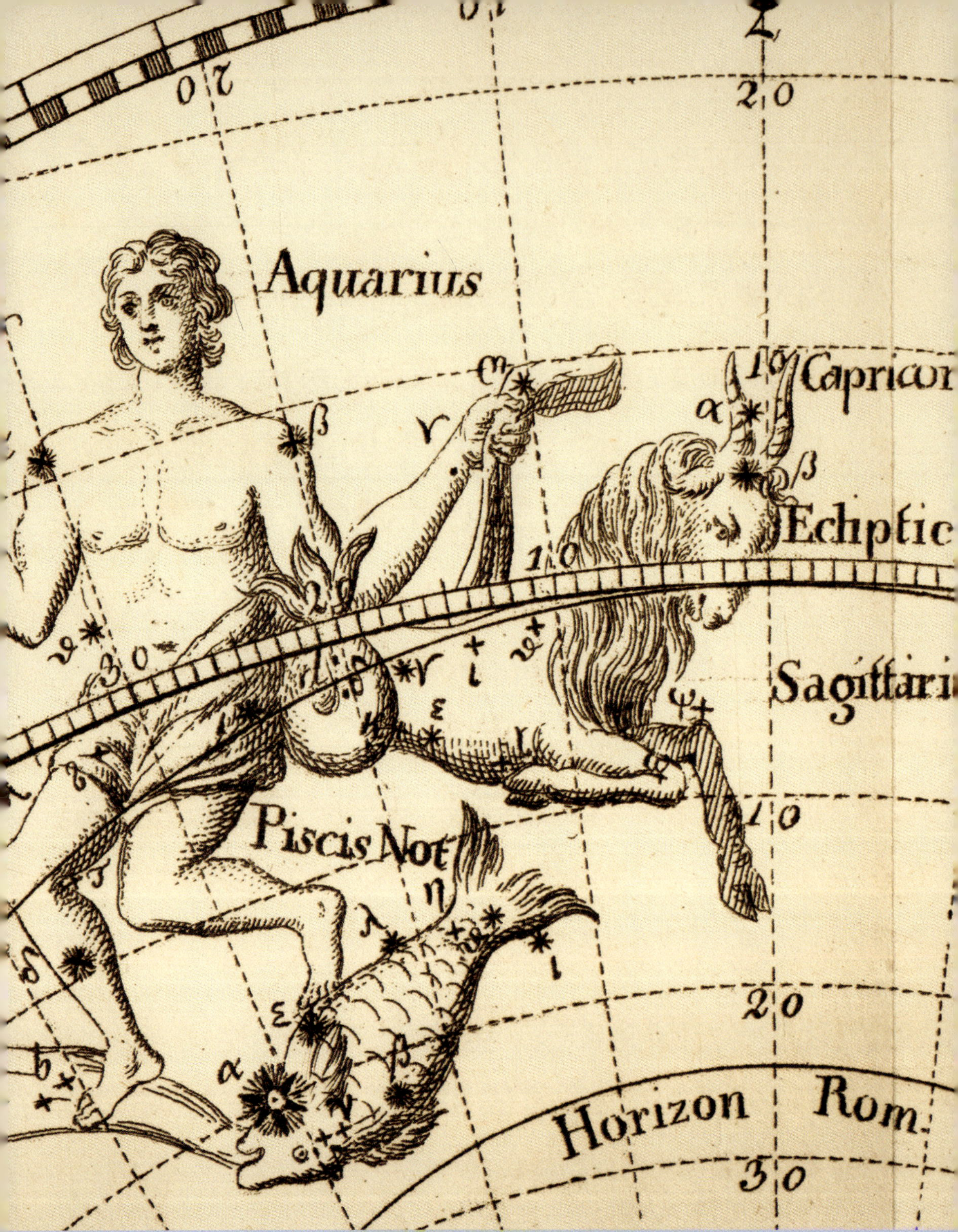
Aquarius
Ecliptic
Piscis Not
Horizon Rom.

Long ago, people in Babylon and Sumer wrote about the constellation. They called it the "goat-fish." The Greeks told stories about it, too.

FAST FACT

The name Capricornus comes from the Latin word for "goat."

◀ Capricornus is near several other water-based constellations.

One story was about a goat that took care of the god Zeus when he was a baby. Another story was about the god Pan. He had the body of a goat.

One Greek myth says a goat named Amalthea fed Zeus when he was a baby.

Pan was a Greek god linked to shepherds and nature. He also played music.

ESCAPE

One story says Pan warned the gods about a monster. To hide, Pan jumped into a river. He turned his lower half into a fish. To thank Pan, Zeus made him into a constellation.

CHAPTER 2

THE ZODIAC

There are 12 **zodiac** signs. Each sign is based on a constellation. Together, they form a cycle. Capricorn is the 10th sign. It's paired with Capricornus.

The first sign of the zodiac is Aries. Pisces is the last sign.

Capricorn's time starts around December 22. It ends around January 19.

START OF WINTER

In the northern **hemisphere**, the **winter solstice** comes in December. It has the longest night and shortest day. It marks the beginning of winter. Capricorn also starts on this day.

Signs that start seasons, such as Capricorn, are called cardinal signs.

In astrology, zodiac signs are said to shape people's lives. People find their signs based on when they were born. Some people read **horoscopes**, too.

Horoscopes give people advice about what to do based on their zodiac signs.

FAST FACT

The zodiac sign that a person was born during is known as their sun sign.

If a horoscope says that something bad will happen, some people may feel trapped.

CHAPTER 3

ABOUT CAPRICORN

In astrology, ruling planets are said to shape how people act. Capricorn's ruling planet is Saturn. This planet is linked with rules and order.

The planet Saturn is named after a Roman god. He was said to control farming, seasons, and time.

Each sign is matched with an **element**. Capricorn's is earth. In astrology, earth signs are said to be **practical**.

FAST FACT

Each element goes with three zodiac signs. Taurus and Virgo are the other earth signs.

Every fourth zodiac sign has the same element.

Water
Fire
Earth
Air
ARIES
TAURUS
GEMINI
CANCER
LEO
VIRGO
LIBRA
SCORPIO
SAGITTARIUS
CAPRICORN
AQUARIUS
PISCES

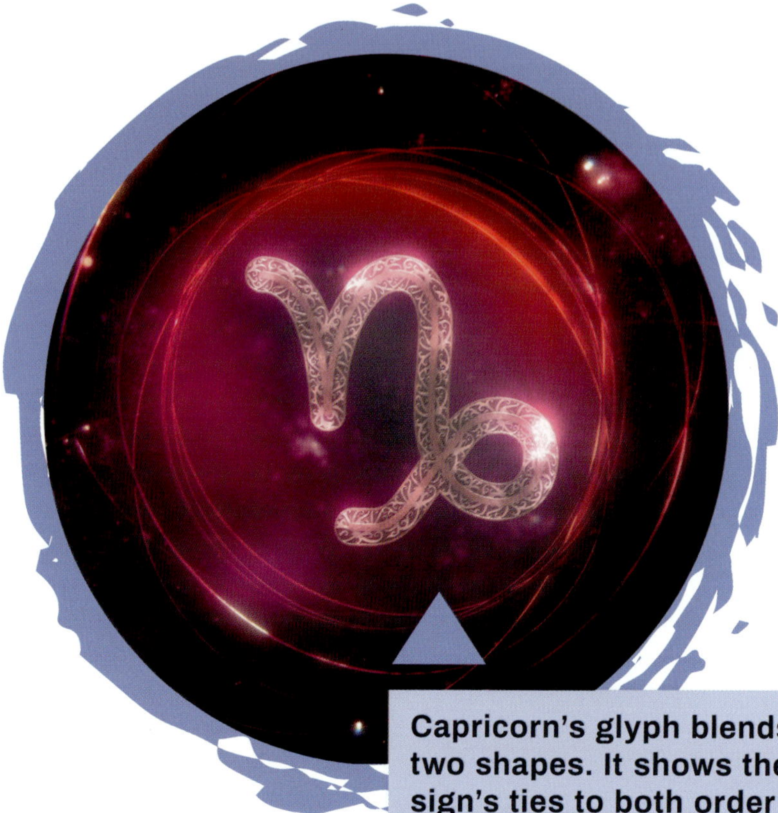

Capricorn's glyph blends two shapes. It shows the sign's ties to both order and feelings.

Each sign also has a **glyph**. Capricorn's looks like a V and a loop. The V is like a goat's hoof or the hair on its chin. The loop is for the fish tail.

HIDDEN HUMOR

Like the sea-goat constellation, Capricorns often have two sides. They can be tough and serious. But many have a fun and playful side, too.

In astrology, water is a symbol of emotion. Signs with ties to water are said to be good at dealing with feelings.

CHAPTER 4

GOING FOR GOALS

In astrology, Capricorns are described as rule followers. They want to do things the right way. They like to plan ahead. And they try to be on time.

Capricorns may use lists and charts to keep track of their plans.

Many Capricorns love to stay busy. They often set lots of goals. They may also have high standards. They expect a lot from themselves and others.

HARD WORKERS

In astrology, Capricorns are hard workers. And they don't give up easily. Some famous Capricorns have these traits. LeBron James is one. Michelle Obama is another.

LeBron James is one of the best basketball players ever. He trained hard to build his skills.

Many Capricorns help their friends solve problems.

Capricorns can be blunt. They say what they think. This can make them seem cold or uncaring. But Capricorns are loyal friends. People can count on them for help and support.

FAST FACT

Capricorns often give good advice.

Capricorns may work as consultants. In these jobs, they help companies find ways to improve.

COMPREHENSION QUESTIONS

Write your answers on a separate piece of paper.

1. Write a few sentences explaining the main ideas of Chapter 4.

2. Do you make lots of goals for yourself? Why or why not?

3. When does Capricorn's time start?

- **A.** December 10
- **B.** December 22
- **C.** January 19

4. How might planning ahead relate to following rules?

- **A.** It makes people more likely to be surprised.
- **B.** It lets people spend less time thinking about how to do things.
- **C.** It gives people time to make sure they do things the right way.

5. What does **standards** mean in this book?

*They may also have high **standards**. They expect a lot from themselves and others.*

A. facts that people learn by reading
B. ideas about how people should act
C. places that people can go

6. What does **loyal** mean in this book?

*But Capricorns are **loyal** friends. People can count on them for help and support.*

A. faithful and true
B. mean and rude
C. fun but fake

Answer key on page 32.

GLOSSARY

constellation
A group of stars that form a shape.

element
One of four forces (air, earth, fire, or water) that each zodiac sign is matched with and said to be shaped by.

glyph
A shape that stands for a word or idea.

hemisphere
One half of planet Earth.

horoscopes
Predictions of the future based on when people were born.

practical
Good at knowing what to do and then doing it.

winter solstice
The day each year when one of Earth's poles is tilted farthest from the sun.

zodiac
The set of 12 signs used in astrology, based on a part of the sky that the sun appears to move through each year.

TO LEARN MORE

BOOKS

Betts, Bruce. *Saturn: The Ringed Planet*. Lerner Publications, 2025.

Loh-Hagan, Virginia. *Star Signs*. Cherry Lake Publishing, 2021.

Nargi, Lela. *Mysteries of the Constellations*. Capstone Publishing, 2021.

ONLINE RESOURCES

Visit **www.apexeditions.com** to find links and resources related to this title.

ABOUT THE AUTHOR

Abby Doty is a writer, editor, and booklover from Minnesota. Her sun sign is Aquarius.

INDEX

ANSWER KEY:

1. Answers will vary; 2. Answers will vary; 3. B; 4. C; 5. B; 6. A